Allie's Ballet Alphabet Book

Judy John-Baptiste

This book belongs to:

.... ELLE Lofin ....

....

....

A Arabesque

A ballet position on one leg

B Battement Tendu

Stretched (leg)

C Curtsey

A female bow to say thank you

D Demi Plié

A half bend of the legs with the heels on the floor

E Echappé

To escape. A jump out to second (an open) position

F Fifth Position

Basic ballet position for the arms and legs

G Grand Plié

A deep knee bend from 1st, 2nd 3rd, 4th, or 5th position

H Hop

A jump on one leg, known in ballet as temps levé

I   Italy

Ballet started in Italy in the fifteenth century

J Jeté

To throw. A jump from one foot to the other

K   Knots

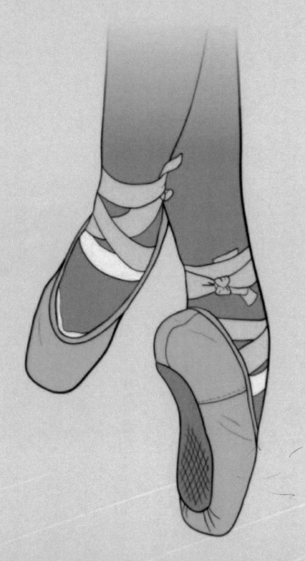

Knots are carefully tied so pointe shoes are
secure when dancing on stage

L Leotard

Dance wear used for ballet practice

M Mime

Using the face and body to express something in ballet

N Notation

A method used to write dance movements

O Ouvert

Open body positions

P Pirouette

A turn of the body on one foot

Q | Quatre

Four. Pas de quatre is a dance for four ballet dancers

R Relevé

To raise or lift; normally the heels off the floor

S   Sauté

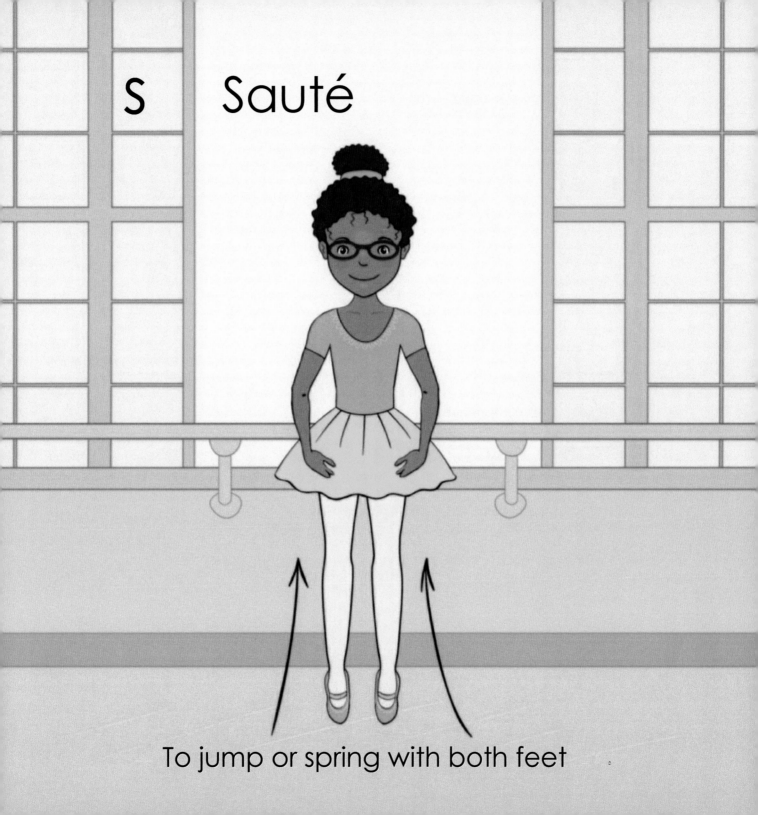

To jump or spring with both feet

T Tutu

A classical ballet skirt with an attached bodice

U   Upstage

Stage direction referring to the back of
a theatre stage

V Variation

A solo dance

W Warm Up

Physical exercises to prepare the body
for ballet dancing

X eXit

STAGE EXIT

Door leading away from the theatre stage

Y You

A classical mime gesture

Z   cZardas

Hungarian folk dance used in ballet

For other books by the author please refer to the website
www.teachingballetcreatively.com

Made in the USA
Middletown, DE
30 May 2020